Joy

For Pink —
The best of
the best I ever.
— Cal

In The Clearing Stands a Boxer

A Pugilist's Poetry Journal

By G.A. Cuddy

Introduction

When I first heard about Haymakers for Hope, I was overtaken with two conflicting emotions: excitement and trepidation.

The latter, of course, was natural considering the fact that few of us will ever box three two-minute rounds in a ring at The House of Blues in Boston in front of 1,500 screaming fans. The former, however, was aided and abetted by Jimmy McGrail, a friend from Charlestown who competed at the 2012 event and would become my mentor for this challenge. After listening to his stories about training and the amazing group of people associated with Haymakers for Hope, I was hooked.

Soon, I learned that two friends-of-friends had fought in previous years and that an acquaintance of mine was also signed up for this year's card. I have done some crazy athletic stunts in the past, but this one had to be the most daring. Whatever bravery I needed to muster, though, paled in comparison to the struggles of several people I know who have battled cancer in the past and are fighting for their lives now. I boxed for them because they have inspired me with courage and candor throughout their treatments and recoveries. Lyn Ackerly, this one was for you!

Beyond the personal test of conditioning oneself for a bout, it was the mission of supporting The Jimmy Fund and The Dana-Farber Cancer Institute that made taking a few punches all the more rewarding. I was fortunate to get into the ring with fellow participants Matt Smith, Maria Tedeschi, Judd Smith, Michelle Kalas, and Ned Hare - and to spar with a great boxer like Jesse Rasid - at Quietman Sports Gym under the direction of our trainer, Dan Parks. We did our best to make one another better and collectively raised over $40K to fight cancer.

This poetry journal/journey details the emotions of a five-month, irreproducible saga and includes photographs of and commentary from many of the Boston '13 boxers. Best of all, part of the proceeds from sales will benefit Haymakers for Hope.

G.A. Cuddy

About Haymakers for Hope

Haymakers for Hope is an official 501(c)(3) charity organization that was founded in the Fall of 2009 by Julie Anne Kelly and Andrew Myerson. Since its inception, over $1M has been raised for The Dana-Farber Cancer Institute, The Jimmy Fund, and other cancer-related hospitals and research facilities.

For further information and to make a donation, please visit the organization's web site at haymakersforhope.org.

Follow on Twitter: @Haymakers4Hope

Acknowledgements

Cover photograph courtesy of Jill Person.

Person + Killian Photography
251 Newbury Street
Boston, MA 02116
617.236.1662
personkillian.com
Follow on Twitter: @PersonKillian

All other photographs courtesy of Haymakers for Hope and Holly Myerson.

Social Media

Follow on Twitter: @StandsABoxer

For Deb Barry

Contents

Cover Your Ears, Son
The Torrey
Our Table
Mikhaila
Forty-Seven Across
Don't Bang The Drum
April 15
Profiles in Carnage
Blizzard '13
The Buckley School
No Physical Contact on Main Street
Haiku, Thank You, Joe
Teufelshunden
Ends in H
Andrea Black
Maith Thú
Who Are These People?
Restitution
Just Very Dear Friends
Toonies
Three If By Fist
Byron's Lament
McHaiKusick
Milena KO/1
June 4, 2014

Boxer G.A. Cuddy

Cover Your Ears, Son

Gesture, posture, boast.
Garish mechanisms all,
mere projections of a frightened, abandoned boy.
"With that mind, he could have done anything he wanted,"
they said.
"All he had to do was apply himself,"
they said.
But it was only love from those he wanted love from most
that he desired.
Concussions of youth, alcohol, drugs,
excuses, they will say,
or perhaps contributors to the abyss of the soul,
one already gutted by tragedy.
The scars, four-ply thick
reopened by throbbing nightmares
and tear-stained pillows in the morning.
Each sun's rising the reminder
of every glove that laid him down
or cut him 'til he cried out.
Bloodied knuckles the trophies,
raised to the heavens and defiant
with accompanying sanguine flow
from lip and nose.
A body heals from the beatings,
a heart never will.

Why am I here on a Thursday and not at the bar?
Boxer Ned Hare

The Torrey

My feigned disinterest - such a failure
for sonnets from the heart claim otherwise,
yet all the evidence one may conjure
seeks to find its shy, wonderful disguise.
Amazing how a smile can warm the heart,
with eyes that tell of days in goodness spent
and each word from her lips can cause sparks
to leave one no objection or dissent.
Attention comes her way and rightly so,
an outer beauty, Aphrodite-like
yet, better still, a soul's erupting flow
cascading over meek and those with might.
Writing now, such bravery, by candle,
shaken by an honesty untangled.

I knew the required dedication level would be high, but the work came easy as I saw the financial support my colleagues, friends, and family were willing to offer. A close friend provided additional incentive as I watched his battle with throat and lung cancer, one he now appears to be winning. I wear his name on my shoes as a reminder of his fight. I have come to appreciate the mental challenge of the boxing experience. I learned that controlling emotion and breathing were attributes necessary to achieve success. I have embraced the need to stay calm and controlled in the face of physical challenge. That has allowed me to literally slow time while I'm in the ring.
Boxer Brian Driscoll

Our Table

Shall we try a Petrarchan sonnet now?
Since I reside in the back of your mind
while you are constant in my heart so kind
a fertile field for love I must plow.
But what lets you stick out from the crowd?
A jukebox choice makes my red knuckles grind
hoisting ale to lips wishing you were mine
yet erecting walls like a fool, so proud.
Down your block I still gaze in wonderment
hands on hips, exhausted, so much longing
sweat-burned eyes from sprints to the monument
with the Ronettes' "Do I Love You?" buzzing.
Which way to turn, now my predicament
each aspect of you so damn disarming.

One song called you the poet of my heart
another recommended you smile,
these lyrics remind me of you, each part,
your name inspiring all the while.
Wandering nearby, collecting pebbles
desiring the chance to be with you,
exploring you on so many levels
from sun's rise until the longest day's through.
Your head nestled upon my shoulder, snug
as each touch spreads warmth throughout our bodies
legs interwoven, eyes fixed: the best drug
to remove boundaries, we are set free.
My thoughts - for one week - strictly about you,
my hope - for all time - the same will be true.

This experience has proven that people have so much good in and so much heart, and I am so grateful to get to participate. I also feel really, really good about being able to project my energies and sweat towards such a good cause. When I'm in the ring, I'm terrified. I've got a lot of stuff going on in my brain, and I'm trying to quiet it all down (feet/hands up, move your head, relax). I get butterflies and I just keep trying to breathe through them. But I also feel great - I like how things flow, I like feeling a natural combo, I like when I get tagged a little and I come back strong, I like watching the other guy's hands and trying to see what's next. So it's a giddy, happy terror.
Boxer Minh-Chau Le

Mikhaila

I still remember my first college love.
How could I not? It was volatile.
Our hearts fit together like hands in gloves
but our fights progressed in a rabid style.
Never have I ever hit a woman,
(I write this under a blue stripe marlin!)
nor would I, as it would be inhuman,
she was the first I ever called darlin'.
Pushed her down on the bed several times
laughed out loud as she tried to hit me back
when we started dating she bought my lines
later I threatened to give her a crack.
Immature. What came over me back then?
Teenage love and sex with her best friends.

The ring is an experience words can't describe. It's both a sanctuary and a death trap. I signed up for this fight to learn about myself and how I feel about boxing. One of my trainers explained that it's something I enjoy and get pleasure out of, so "embrace the entire experience - especially the nervousness and anxiety." I don't believe in limits and this experience has been a test of that.
Boxer Raf Montes

Forty-Seven Across

Orange Line train commuters' downward glances
meet feet that shuffle over dirty floors
when eyes are not closed ruing the chances
of opportunities lost and closed doors.
Unfinished crossword puzzles sit on laps
and earphones exclude the conductor's call
for upcoming stations and minding gaps
heavy breathing creates a deathly pall.
Construction workers' boots bear molten dust
next to businessmen in suits crisply pressed
as bums sleep off a night of drunken lust
and schoolgirls study for a Latin test.
Someone just stood too close to my own space
gripping the bar I shield my brave face.

It's not so much the training experience but what has led me here. My dad's side of the family has been hit hard by cancer (lost my grandfather and two aunts, while an uncle and cousin are currently battling it). On my mother's side, my uncle passed a year ago. I will try to do my part with anything fighting cancer and that's why I'm doing this fight. Boxing in Haymakers for Hope will be my way of saying thank you, I love you, and hoping the money raised will make a difference in at least one person's life.
Boxer Marco Bossolo

Don't Bang The Drum

They all think you're an Irish band, an Irishman
in floppy hat and velour coat
festooned with flags, rags, and ferryboats,
scimitars and scarves.
But I knew different, studied you I did,
when you were a young man, and I was just a kid.

Summer job, high school money earned
for an eight mile round-trip rainy walk to buy your album,
wrapped in a double bag, popped myself a Valium
then picked the lint off the turntable needle.
Scottish fire-igniter of my soul, setting me aglow
with your Celtic 'twang down life's littered road.

That was the river, this is the sea
for pagans and righteous fellows, felled,
and lyrics that deep within your heart dwell
came to life in my headphones nightly.
Suddenly, at seventeen, empty pockets mattered not,
for this wandering waterboy's vibrant wanderlust.

It was an amazing four-month experience with the hard training culminating on fight night. For me, with no boxing experience going in, it was a great chance to train with some of the best in the sport, learn tons about myself, and work towards a great goal in the process. It's rare you're afforded an opportunity like that - so glad I threw my hat into the ring!
Boxer Bubba Hagood

April 15

The blasts are not what I remember.
Instead, the whoosh of white-jacketed medical personnel
sprinting past my left shoulder
into danger, into the unknown on Boylston Street,
administering immediate action to start the breathing and stop the bleeding.
Gettysburg.
Oh, how many lives they saved!
Limbs and skin torn asunder,
into the shock of the moment, so many stood there in wonderment
frozen at first, then responding
comforting the tears, hugging the collapsed
amid broken glass and hearts,
no one knew how much time had lapsed.
We ran to them as they ran to us,
dazed, confused
terror wrought upon innocents again.

It was an exciting event and the shots I took - and there were plenty of them - were worth it to raise money and awareness for cancer research. Thanks to Haymakers for Hope, Nonantum Boxing Club, and all of my fellow competitors.
Boxer Tom Sheehan

Profiles in Carnage

So many times I've stood on the platform at Back Bay Station
ready to fling my body into the path
of an oncoming Orange Line train
just like the months in Williamsburg
when I wanted to jump out of Pink's tenth floor loft window
to hit the pavement below in front of the Hasidic lumber supply
warehouse.
But my fear was the part about not finding out what happens next in life:
the next round, when the bell rings/tolls.
Perhaps this is not my death, but the death of vanity
or the ultimate form of self-criticism
and escapism unlike the ring, where there is no escape
from an opponent's fists.
One must answer that damn bell
with every hit absorbed and given
as it rings again and one's enthusiasm for the next round
remains toiling for us all,
not just at the station for the next train.

When I am training, I am thinking about learning the skills needed to win in order to make my gym, my trainer, myself, and the people who supported me with donations proud. I am honored to be able to do something I love to do and have it benefit such a great cause. My funds are now going to a friend's charity (Martha C. Kinnecom Primary Peritoneal Cancer Foundation). My childhood friend, Kim, lost her mom to this unfamiliar type of cancer and her family is dedicated to increasing knowledge and serving as advocates for patients with peritoneal cancer. I, like many, have had family members die from cancer, and have known so many people dealing with cancer in some way or another. Fighting for such a great cause...why not?
Boxer Kim Peltier

Blizzard '13

On the Back Bay platform I can see her face
but she looks away as soon as I smile
so I put that smile back into its place
hands in my pockets like a chastised child.
Shoulder brushes with strangers mean little
just like a bumper car duel with drunk friends
now this is my amusement park wild thrill
observing strangers until my ride's end.
Afraid to engage with my gift of gab
afraid to believe that I am worthy
to greet a stranger's wish to share a cab
after a subway ride's ogling spree.
Better to keep to myself again now
alone, making angels on my back in the snow.

As for how I feel in the ring, I'm always a bit nervous. But you tell yourself to be positive, to breathe deeply, and stay confident. That always seems to work until you get thrown in the washing machine, which may be similar to getting hit by a combination of punches. But sometimes, when you're the one connecting on combinations, it can be a flow experience. Boxing looks simple, but when you're both throwing punches and effectively blocking or slipping them, and it's happening at lightning speed, you're synthesizing all these techniques and you realize, "Holy shit, I'm not just fighting anymore, I'm boxing!" As an amateur, these moments where everything's going right in the ring are far outnumbered by moments where your trainer's telling you how much you're doing wrong, but damn those moments of flow are sweet.
Boxer Thomas Mayell

The Buckley School

How did I end up alone, so content?
A cold sandwich with some chips on my couch.
all life's miseries too late to repent
death and heartbreaks like a punch in the mouth.
Walking calm down some dangerous streets
embracing self-destruction at a glance
striding confidently on icy streets
challenging a ruffian's boxer stance.
Roxy Music albums litter my floor
a broken neon light I stole draws dust
muddy shoes and baseball hats near the door
and never-sent sonnets speckled with lust.
Let us paint the picture for you clearly
not an "I love you" in six years, nearly.

Training for this fight has helped me heal on so many levels. I can talk about the people I have lost, their legacies, and their influences as I train with others. I feel stronger emotionally - I now know I can get hit in the face and keep going! I have being eating a largely vegan diet and have lost twenty pounds while getting healthier in body as well as mind and reducing my own risk of cancer.

Boxing is a religion in my family and one of my great-uncles was a professional fighter and referee, so it has been great to experience this sport firsthand. My father's last words to me were "It's a good thing you are a fighter," and I am striving
to live up to that affirmation.
Boxer Michelle Kalas

No Physical Contact on Main Street

Sullivan's Pub in Charlestown I fear
may succumb to a yuppie invasion
but Paulie and Jackie still serve cold beer
amid the growing gentrification.
Hearty Gaelic anthems on the jukebox
tell of rebels in Belfast and Derry
singing together above idle talk
we toast "Sláinte!" and order whiskey.
A man left alone here may write a poem
seated in a booth away from others
head down, focused, in a creative zone
knowing a local has his back covered.
We want these good times to last forever
but, like Irish peace, a vain endeavor.

For me, the training was incredibly visceral experience of less being more: less effort, more force. less strain, more power. less movement, more evasiveness, less aggression, more results. It was also an introduction to an incredibly caring community of people committed to taking on big scary things - cancer, boxing - and being thoughtful and generous and open with their experiences.
Boxer Joe Panepinto

Haiku, Thank You, Joe

Sinewy tissues
expended to their limits
as the sweat pours down.

Slithery movements
my shadow on a gym's wall
dancing, prancing heart.

Lie-la-lie, he sang.
In the clearing? A boxer.
Boston's aging boy.

Proud to be bested
by another gentleman
fighting for this cause.

Two hands raised as one
victory in a fair fight,
cancer's met its match.

The greatest honor of my life was serving the United States of America as a member of the Marine Corps. The sacrifice and dedication necessary was made simple knowing that it was a prerequisite for the privilege to protect our country. I have been similarly driven in preparing for the Haymakers for Hope event, one of so many amazing grassroots efforts focused on eradicating cancer. It was another tremendous honor to be one of the athletes putting their reputation and facial bone structure on the line to raise money for such a great cause. The friends I have made during this process and the inspirational stories I've heard from cancer victims and survivors has made the overall experience one of the best in my life. It wouldn't be possible without the tremendous efforts of the event organizers and the incredible trainers at Peter Welch's Gym. I can't thank them enough for all their efforts.
Boxer Allen Potts

Teufelshunden

Shook the hand of me twenty years ago
a young Marine so vibrant with hopes high
remembering the swagger like a pro
two decades on a quite different guy.
Strong veiny forearms from pull-ups and guns
high and tight haircut, rosy face, big smile
connected by boot camp stories of fun
like humping Mount Motherfucker's miles.
"Shipping off tomorrow," he said to me,
"a few more texts to family and friends."
The bartender gave him a beer for free
and I worried that his young life might end.
These are the boys who keep us safe at night
they are the men our government makes fight.

This was probably one of the most difficult things I have ever done, not to mention the most anxiety-producing experience of my life. But knowing that I was doing it for a good cause, and there were more than two dozen other people experiencing these same feelings, made the entire thing worthwhile. Would I change a few things about my training experience? Yes. I wish I was a bit more aggressive and confident in my ability to fight. It wasn't about winning or losing for me the night of the fight, it was about proving to myself that I could get in the ring with an opponent, in front of tons of people, and stick through the entire six minutes and give it my all. The entire four months seemed stressful as it went on, but by the time I stepped out of the ring on fight night, I felt like I had truly achieved something awesome, and it made every bloody day, every blow to the head, every shot to the ribs worth it.
Boxer Steve Annear

Ends in H

Another sonnet for a stranger
gets the same response as the last three.
Truth: I have sent the same poem to different women
but not to Sarah,
my heart too entwined in the dream of being with her.
Stealing her away from her boyfriend named Romeo or Romero
or whatever the fuck his name happens to be.
All advice from friends to stay away, and I do, that's fine
but not out of respect for them
only for her
Not my type.
Not my style.
Yet, perfect for me. Everything for me
I constructed crossword puzzles for her, for Christ's sake!
(First time I've ever written "For Christ's sake!")
She is a challenge, like so many others,
but I was in foolhardy control.
I ceased contact.
I dedicated my fight to her.
I liked her.

Training for this event has been life-altering for me. I've met some great people and definitely stepped out of my comfort zone; and I get the chance to train for a boxing match next to my future wife a month before our wedding. Watching her step into the ring is even more nerve-racking than having to face my own opponent. When I think about what we are fighting for, it gives me strength. My sister-in-law was recently diagnosed with breast cancer and has responded almost 100% through chemotherapy, but it changed her and my brother's lives. My brother's family's perseverance throughout months of treatment and tough news gave me the strength to ignore my bloody noses, and bruised cheek bones and to keep on punching. I know getting into the boxing ring is that much easier than fighting cancer, but I'll do my part and hopefully what I'm doing will help us find a cure.
Boxer Judd Smith

Andrea Black

How does one bring
a boxer to his knees
without repeated blows
to the torso and head,
round by round,
until an inevitable collapse occurs?
In her case, easy!
A smile
or a look directly into my eyes
that numbs and freezes
better than any opponent's feint
and devastates
more than any combination of uppercuts.

Thunderstruck, not by a phantom punch
but by lithe movements
as gentle as dew upon daffodils
that clings to drooping edges
until sunlight arrives.

She is everything good in the world:
a chocolate malt at an amusement park,
buttered popcorn at a movie theater,
Messi on the ball,
Ali on his toes.

From which garden do those like Andrea Black bloom?
Only heaven knows.

I started out thinking it would be a good test of my "aging" athleticism and a good reason to step up my workouts to better my conditioning and shape. I had no idea as to the personal satisfaction the experience would give back. I can honestly say it has been one of the most rewarding endeavors I've ever undertaken – my proudest achievement is the amount of money that I was able to raise for this great cause, and the fact that my contributor totaled seventy-four - a much greater turnout than I thought I would get. I got to fight on a stage in front of over a thousand people and I have gained a tremendous amount of respect for those that have preceded us. Through the bloody noses, the fat lips, the black eyes, and the constant muscle aches, I never stopped enjoying it! Thank you to Julie and Andrew, Dave, and Holly – you are doing wonderful work and I'm extremely proud to be associated with Haymakers for Hope.
Boxer Hugh Deery

Maith Thú

A kind bricklayer just bought me a pint
cold, soothing Bass ale in a frosted glass
still waiting for a gal I met last night
who I kissed on the cheek, inspiring lass.
The mutual exchange of buying rounds
a rite of passage for the Irishman
not just the measure of how much you pound
but the slap on the back from priest and con.
Someone's quarter just played The Galway Girl,
bloody hell! Another pint's come my way
I hear the door open, hope it's her
instead, a boyo from County Mayo.
Regrets that I haven't been here for years
Playing catch up on drinks and the good cheer.

Wow, that actually hurt!
Boxer Nick Mathews

Who Are These People?

One pair of jeans, one pair of khaki pants
black leather boots and tennis shoes with holes
old iPod and phone, coolness? Not a chance.
Going to places where the riff-raff bowls.
Drunk cab rides that end when the cash runs out
walking strange blocks in the rain acting sober
cops pass and eyeball just another lout
only good luck is a crack stepped over.
Exempt from preparation for success
dropping out no longer so romantic
drugs, booze, and women to excess
now alone surviving as an addict.
With lottery ticket superstitions
subway riders glance with strict derision.

I really appreciated all of the help from the trainers at Peter Welch's Gym. They did a great job not only getting me into physical condition to do this but also into the mental condition to do it. It was a pleasure working with the other boxers in the gym. I was always apprehensive to spar because I always thought that everyone had a ton of experience. Once I tried it, I realized that a lot of them were also new to it and even the ones that had been training for a while ended up being very helpful with me. This was something I had always wanted to do but was always a little scared. I am grateful for being asked to participate and for everyone that helped me get through it. I am also grateful for Tom Sheehan - he put up a great fight and I have a lot of respect for him and the other fighters. It's not easy preparing and going in there for three rounds.
Boxer Alex Winston

Restitution

Just imaginary conversations
in the mind of an awkward little boy
who wanted to find a place for his throne
and finally feel that thing we call joy.
Out of date glasses on a Roman nose
with a hump and a bend from losing fights
outnumbered, alone, in tattered clothes
hitching a ride home, the end of his nights.
No glory in the emotional loss
for an abandoned, shy man in the rain
with red face afire and graying hair tossed
seeking out dangerous streets to find pain.
Nailing up a cross and hoisting his fists
heading directly into an abyss.

It was an experience that involved late nights of sparring and early morning runs. From the bloody noses and black eyes to cut up knuckles and workouts that made me gasp for air, I wouldn't change a thing about it!
Boxer Eric Pellegrini

Just Very Dear Friends

Whispering, often, to photographs of you
Wishing, hoping, that you will be alive next to me
I relate dreams and desires, earthly bound
Your cheek on my chest, nestled
Sensing a longing heart nearby.
Bodies entwined, coiled, ready to strike
Brought together as one, mutually charmed
These dreams recur each night, each morning
Unjust to define with mere words
A shivering collapse of joy together.
How brash these thoughts to a stranger
Harsh to those protected, fearful souls
The unwilling to dare always lose hope
Yet inside of you, a world's joy rediscovered
A sweet, robust, savory breath of passion.

I hate getting punched in the face. And the forehead, and the side of the head, or anywhere really. Before training began I was confident I could handle the physical task of getting back into shape. Recently, I have realized how intricate training to be a boxer is. It's about being able to adapt to the situation and read your opponent's every move in order to find that perfect attack. Fighting for such a great cause makes it easy to step back into the ring for another sparring match, or another session on the mitts. Our willingness to win and to keep fighting comes from the people we know who are fighting a completely different battle. In training, I try to focus on what I can control. I can control how much effort I put forth. I can't tell you how much strength I draw from my training partners George, Matt, and my fiancé, Judd. I draw strength from my trainer, Dan. But, most importantly I draw strength from my family and friends who will not give up in their fight against cancer. At the end of the day the pain from a few punches to the face is nothing compared to weeks of treatments, surgeries, or losing a loved one.
Boxer Maria Tedeschi

Toonies

Callous strangers enter my local pub
then bemoan the cash only policy
oblivious to the dynamic club
of an Irish family's hearty tree.
Asking for chardonnay instead of beer
scoffing at holiday decorations
eyes buried in smart phones absent of cheer
unknowingly drawing consternation.
Phony banker crooks with argyle socks
lock-jawed from turtlenecks and fleece scarves
immune to a life working on the docks
so close to getting their jugulars carved.
Just pay for your drinks and keep your mouths shut
you'll never fit in, you don't have the guts.

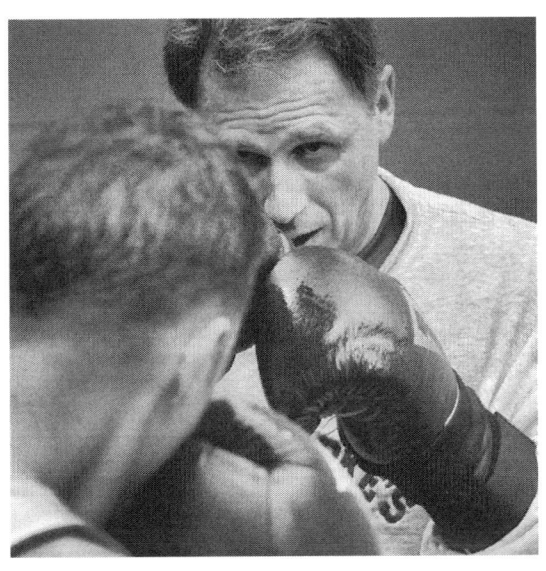

I was surprised, in the weeks leading up to the fight, that I thought I couldn't wait for this to end. The Friday night sparring matches, followed by early Saturday morning training and sparring again, then Sunday training, Monday training, finally Tuesday night off and back in on Wednesday made for an exhausting week. Sparring with our trainer and wondering is this one of the nights he teaches you how to take a punch - bloody noses, locked jaws, and a broken rib. Constantly thinking about the fight, every time you're in front of the mirror is an opportunity to shadow box for a couple of minutes, lying awake at night working out the combinations. Hundreds of sit-ups, squats, and push-ups! Now that it's over, I miss it. I can't wait to get back to the gym again. I'm looking forward to sparring, hitting, getting hit, the pain, the adrenaline rush, the butterflies. I'm hooked and I can't believe it.
Boxer Robin Monleon

Three If By Fist

Living in the shadows of Bunker Hill
I sleep where patriots marched to fight
brave men with muskets and iron-forged wills
not knowing if they would survive the night.
We take their sacrifices for granted
Always forgetting them, I know I do.
They died to earn our rights, eternal in granite
such valor in today's world is all moot.
Scrambling behind bushes, rifles raised
Red coats in their sights, knees and feet in mud
charging the cannons through morning's gray haze
sacrificing for a cause with their blood.
And I rest my head on a soft pillow
safe from smoke on a hill that once billowed

Tourists snap photos of Old Ironsides
then turn to walk the Freedom Trail's path.
Longing for glory in their boring lives
with no conception of history's wrath.
Mangled hands and legs with sad, broken hearts
confined to chair or bed or walking stick
poisoned by medicine from their care's start
eye patches stained with tears, fresh wounds to lick.
Family letters come less and less often
past comrades in arms die alone and broke
medals, ribbons do little to soften
traumatic memories that hold no hope.
Volunteers work at the shelter one time
thanks for your service, lend me a dime.

Training for my first competitive boxing match was an incredible experience, both physically and mentally. While I anticipated the physical demands required to transform my body into fighting shape, I didn't fully appreciate the mental challenges that ultimately presented themselves - learning how to breathe, manage adrenaline, and battle through injuries. Midway through my training, I discovered that my trainer's mother was battling with cancer, and this became an important part of my journey. Whenever I hit a wall in my preparation, I remembered those people in my life (uncles, aunts, and my trainer's mother) who had and were still battling for their lives. This not only fueled my drive, but also provided me with great meaning and purpose.
Boxer Varun Solan

Byron's Lament

Nobody should care about a poor poet
because he made the choice to be that way
whether he's infamous or hardly known
on deaf ears do fall the words that he says.
Couplets or iambic pentameter
abstract verse meant for his long lost loves
lacking a fair title of Mister or Sir
filling notebooks written under covers.
Bleeding with each word on the yellow page
crying out loud about passion's refrain
blistered and shattered, no dreams at his age
longing for some sort of redemptive gain.
Always an anachronism to most
seeking to satisfy poetry's ghosts.

Still thinking about the girl I met here
at Sullivan's Pub in Charlestown, Mass.
Two weeks ago over beer and good cheer
talking football with an Italian lass.
Adorned with lip gloss and trinkets and scarves
long legs and black boots with a purple shirt
holding my heart at the end of the bar
listening to stories was not rough work.
All verse feel tawdry without her near me
I can close my eyes and smell her right now
and recall kissing her cheek, hand on knee
leaning in closer, an eternal vow.
Absence making the heart grow much fonder
What does she covet? It is this I ponder.

I am a cancer survivor, so this endeavor has had an extraordinary effect upon me both inside and outside of the ring. It was a struggle, at times, to suffer through the extremely difficult workouts at our gym, but I knew that the path I had traveled in the past would prepare me for this moment.

The generosity of my friends and colleagues in raising funds for this charity was remarkable, but I was just as impressed that so many people came to the House of Blues to see my fight and to support the cause. It was an honor to be a participant and I wish the best for all of those who step into the ring for Haymakers for Hope in the future.
Boxer Matt Smith

McHaiKusick

Said move to New York
biggest lie I've ever told
forever, Boston.

Afraid of your eyes
they burn holes right through my soul
mysteries abound.

Oh, Laura, so wise
yet unknowing of the thrills
you provide to all.

I thought Haymakers for Hope was a challenging journey. I found it very rewarding to be a part of something that gives back to those in need. Hopefully, my journey and the journey of the rest of the boxers will aid in cancer research. I feel that H4H was well coordinated and the matchups were fair. I feel honored to be part of the Haymakers for Hope family.
Boxer Renzo Monzon

Melina KO/1

One imagines her sashaying (or dreams about it)
down a lazy street in New Orleans
maybe Madame Tranchepain during balmy August
subtle beads of perspiration gracing her décolletage
whimsically smiling at strangers
who gawk at her radiance.

Each step as smooth as Pavlova and Fonteyn
the opposite of my plodding in a boxing ring
that May night across from Fenway Park
and, then, a glancing wind fluffs her sundress softly
and moves a tuft of her silken hair
lustrous as the sun that glows upon the mighty Mississippi.

I get so nervous in her presence
keeping my hands up to protect myself
from the jabs of her beauty
and the jabs of my opponent
whose haymakers I see coming
unlike those from her, to which we are all blind.

In the fray, I hear nothing
but the beating of my heart
and my lungs, gasping for air
those of my opponent, too,
with the occasional instructions from our trainers
two warriors battling for Helen, for Nefertiti, or for glory.

We carry the reminders
of every glove that laid us down
or cut us 'til we cried out
in our anger and our shame
"We are leaving, we are leaving,"
but inspirations like Melina still remain.

The Poet

G.A. Cuddy is the author of *Where Hash Rules*, a history of Charlie's Sandwich Shoppe in Boston's South End, and lives in Charlestown (MA). He attended the University of California at Los Angeles, served in the United States Marine Corps, has never had a cup of coffee, and considers "mellifluous" his favorite word. *In The Clearing Stands a Boxer* is his first poetry collection.

--

In my mind's eye you're sitting at our table tonight. Or maybe eating a Pop-Tart. I'm sorry for the past week. And for lots more than that. Here's to better timing.

June 14, 2013
10:06 PM

June 4, 2014

Upon a field of poppies I ran
on an unmarked trail
across a vast farmland
with mud on my legs
and wind in my face
in a desperate struggle
to keep a decent pace.
Then, as the nearby trees did loom
I reflected on the poppies' bloom
for the sun-drenched kiss
on a petal moist
and a heart so passionate
for its ultimate choice.
Into the woods
I ventured at speed
through puddles
over logs
while slipping on leaves
my heart beating wildly
as a mist filled the air
time frozen and forgotten
but I had not a care.
Bounding further and faster
thinking only of you
I returned to the expanse
where the flowers all grew
then gazed at the sunset
with its glorious glow
robust and euphoric
like the love I've come to know.

Made in the USA
San Bernardino, CA
18 June 2014